inside Life

INSIDE LIFE
A DOUBLEDAY BOOK 978 0 385 61716 1

Published in Great Britain by Doubleday,
an imprint of Random House Children's Books
A Random House Group Company

This edition published 2009

1 3 5 7 9 10 8 6 4 2

Published to accompany the television series Inside LIFE, first broadcast on
the BBC in 2009.

BBC and the BBC logo are trademarks of the British Broadcasting Corporation
and are used under licence. BBC logo © BBC 1996.

Text copyright © Random House, 2009
The picture credits on p. 92 constitute an extension to this copyright notice.

The right of Doug Hope and Vanessa Coates to be identified as the authors of
this work has been asserted in accordance with the Copyright, Designs and
Patents Act 1988.

RANDOM HOUSE CHILDREN'S BOOKS
61–63 Uxbridge Road, London W5 5SA

www.kidsatrandomhouse.co.uk
www.rbooks.co.uk

Addresses for companies within The Random House Group Limited can be
found at: www.randomhouse.co.uk/offices.htm

THE RANDOM HOUSE GROUP Limited Reg. No. 954009

A CIP catalogue record for this book is available from the British Library.

Printed in Great Britain by Butler Tanner and Dennis, Frome.

inside
Life

Written by Doug Hope and Vanessa Coates

DOUBLEDAY

CONTENTS

TOP SECRET

MISSION:

AGENT:

ALIAS:

MISSION: COMPLETED!

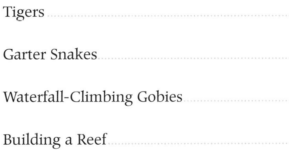

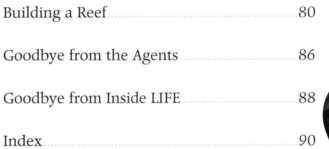

INTRODUCING

LIFE

For such a small word, LIFE covers a lot.

It includes everything from tiny, brainless jellyfish that live in the deepest seas to mighty African elephants and giant redwood trees. It includes every butterfly, beetle and bug, every orang-utan, flower and rock-pool crab, every toadstool, tortoise and tarantula, grass stems, coral, panthers . . . the list goes on and on.

Anything and everything that lives and breathes – including us – is part of LIFE.

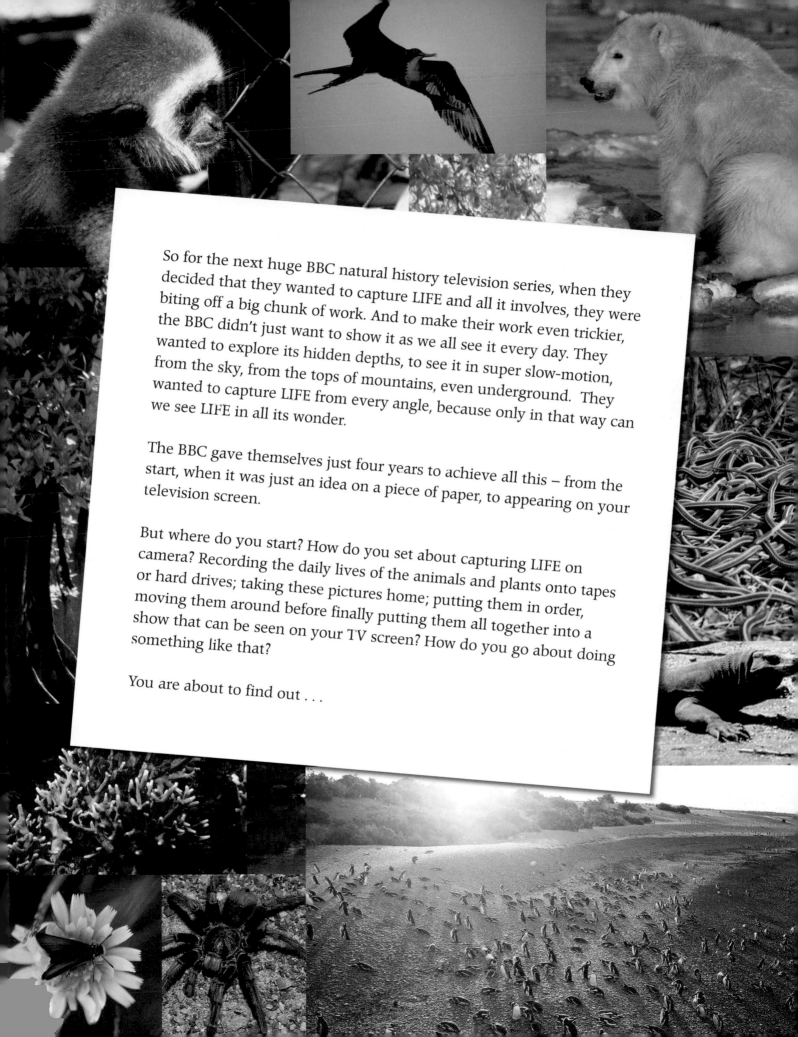

So for the next huge BBC natural history television series, when they decided that they wanted to capture LIFE and all it involves, they were biting off a big chunk of work. And to make their work even trickier, the BBC didn't just want to show it as we all see it every day. They wanted to explore its hidden depths, to see it in super slow-motion, from the sky, from the tops of mountains, even underground. They wanted to capture LIFE from every angle, because only in that way can we see LIFE in all its wonder.

The BBC gave themselves just four years to achieve all this – from the start, when it was just an idea on a piece of paper, to appearing on your television screen.

But where do you start? How do you set about capturing LIFE on camera? Recording the daily lives of the animals and plants onto tapes or hard drives; taking these pictures home; putting them in order, moving them around before finally putting them all together into a show that can be seen on your TV screen? How do you go about doing something like that?

You are about to find out . . .

INTRODUCING

INSIDE LIFE

INSIDE LIFE is the first series of its kind; a CBBC show that is connected with a huge natural history series – a show that gets inside LIFE. But we didn't just want to get behind the scenes to see how these massive wildlife shows are made, we wanted more.

We wanted to get involved. So we sent 10 secret CBBC agents into the field, ready to get hands-on, help out, and be there while it was all happening.

All our agents had applied to be involved in CBBC shows, but none of them knew just what we had in store for them.

MISSION: UK CHALLENGE

TOP SECRET
MISSION: Gibbons
AGENT: Bryony
ALIAS: Bry

TOP SECRET
MISSION: Ring-tailed lemurs
AGENT: Billy
ALIAS: Bill

TOP SECRET
MISSION: Komodo dragons
AGENT: Isobel
ALIAS: Izzy

TOP SECRET
MISSION: Gobies
AGENT: Jacob
ALIAS: Jake

TOP SECRET
MISSION: Frigate birds
AGENT: Gregory
ALIAS: Greg

Each agent was first given a UK challenge. These ranged from learning how to film underwater to researching how to find a Komodo dragon. Each challenge covered part of the process of making a wildlife film from researching to using special equipment.

What none of the agents knew was that this was just the start of their adventures. When they had completed their UK challenge, it was revealed to them that they would be jetting off somewhere in the world to join the LIFE team while they were filming.

Filming is the most important part of making a nature documentary but it can be very time-consuming. You can't direct animals like you can direct actors. They're not giving a performance, they're just living their lives. You can't ask them to repeat that amazing moment when they fight, hunt or fly – you just have to be there when it happens, ready to film, or you'll miss it. That's why it can take up to four years to film a nature documentary.

But before you are in the right place to film, there is a lot of work to do.

MEET THE INSIDE LIFE TEAM

THE AGENTS

JAMES has dreams of being James Bond – he has no idea how close he is going to get!

SCARLET has never been outside the UK before, so what the LIFE team have in store for her is going to be a real adventure . . .

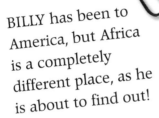

BILLY has been to America, but Africa is a completely different place, as he is about to find out!

GREGORY is a computer gamer – but will this skill help him in his mission?

LOUISE is super-tough, and she needs to be, as she will be heading out to the coldest destination on INSIDE LIFE.

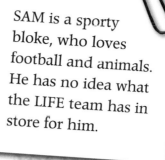

SAM is a sporty bloke, who loves football and animals. He has no idea what the LIFE team has in store for him.

ISOBEL's favourite animal is the ring-tailed lemur, but the animal she's going to meet would eat them for dinner.

BRYONY is a perfect presenter and loves TV. The good news is that she is not afraid of heights – good news for the LIFE team, that is!

JACOB is a really active guy who loves technology – we had the perfect job for him.

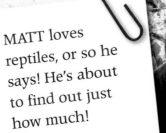

MATT loves reptiles, or so he says! He's about to find out just how much!

THE MISSIONS

NORTH AMERICA

3

8

9

10

SOUTH AMERICA

6

4

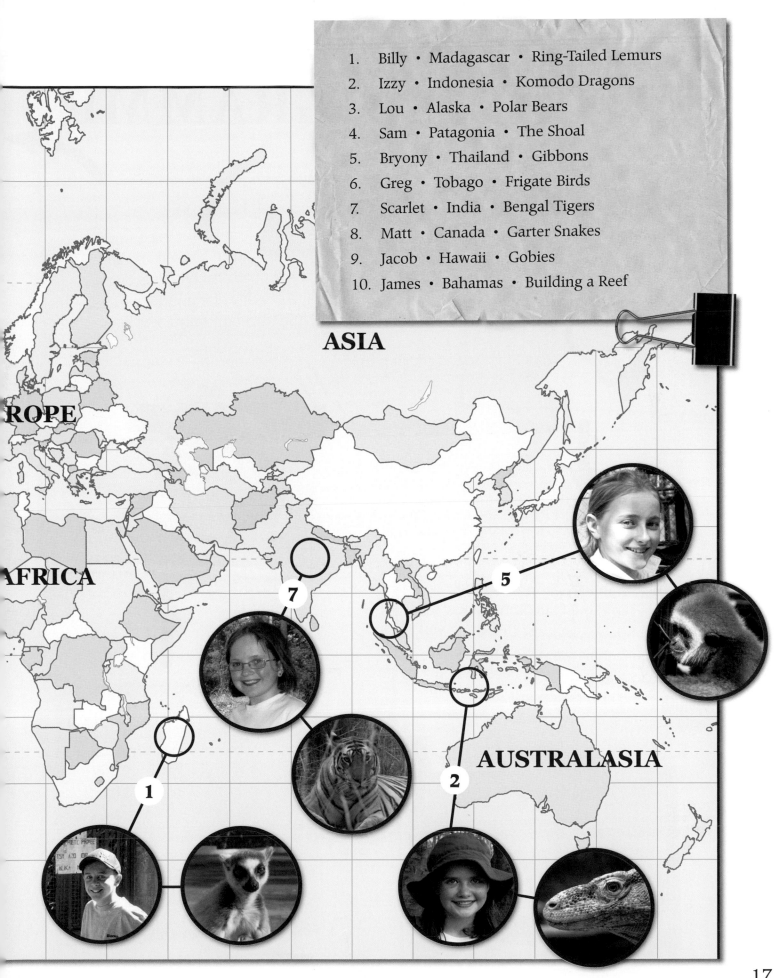

1. Billy • Madagascar • Ring-Tailed Lemurs
2. Izzy • Indonesia • Komodo Dragons
3. Lou • Alaska • Polar Bears
4. Sam • Patagonia • The Shoal
5. Bryony • Thailand • Gibbons
6. Greg • Tobago • Frigate Birds
7. Scarlet • India • Bengal Tigers
8. Matt • Canada • Garter Snakes
9. Jacob • Hawaii • Gobies
10. James • Bahamas • Building a Reef

ASIA

EUROPE

AFRICA

AUSTRALASIA

HOW TO MAKE A NATURE PROGRAMME

The film-making process starts with an idea . . .

FILMING

Once all the details have been worked out, the cameramen booked and all the flights and hotels paid for, it is time to go filming! Some filming trips can last two months, some only a few days.

RESEARCH

If you want to tell a story about how different birds and animals behave in unique and bizarre ways, the first thing you have to do is some research. This means you have to search through books and the internet, and also ask experts, to find out about the latest discoveries and behaviours.

CO-ORDINATION

This is when the producers sit down with the co-ordinators. Together they work out exactly what they can film and where the best places are to do this. They also look at how much money they have to spend on each project.

EDITING

The next process is editing. All the animals have been filmed – there can be several hours of footage for just one animal – and it's up to the editor to watch all the tapes, put them onto the computer and pick the best bits which will go together to make the final sequence you'll see on television.

Then you get to watch it on TV and that is how you make a nature programme!

MUSIC

Now's the time to add the finishing touches. First the film is graded – a clever tool is used on the computer to make the pictures look even more spectacular. Then it's time to add music and sound effects.

THE FINAL MIX

This is the final stage of the filming process. All the pictures and the sounds come together before it is put onto television.

THE CREW

RESEARCHER

This job involves finding the stories that the teams want to film. To do this, they talk to experts and scientists. For wildlife shows, a lot of researchers have a biology or zoology degree. Sometimes researchers get the chance to help film on location.

ASSISTANT PRODUCER

Using information given to them by the researcher, assistant producers select the stories that are going to go into the film. APs, as they are known, also help on location with the filming.

PRODUCER

The producer's job is to write and film the sequences that, with the help of the researcher and the assistant producer, have been selected to be filmed. The producer will, with the help of the editor, put the whole film together. They write a guide script and work out where the music and graphics should go, as well as the order in which the filmed sequences will appear.

EDITOR

Editors work closely with the producer to edit the filmed footage and produce sequences which are then cut and put into the right order. This is all done with computers.

PRODUCTION CO-ORDINATOR

This is a very important job. Production co-ordinators need to make sure that the team have all the right equipment with them as well as visas and permission to film. They also have the tough job of looking after the budget for their programmes.

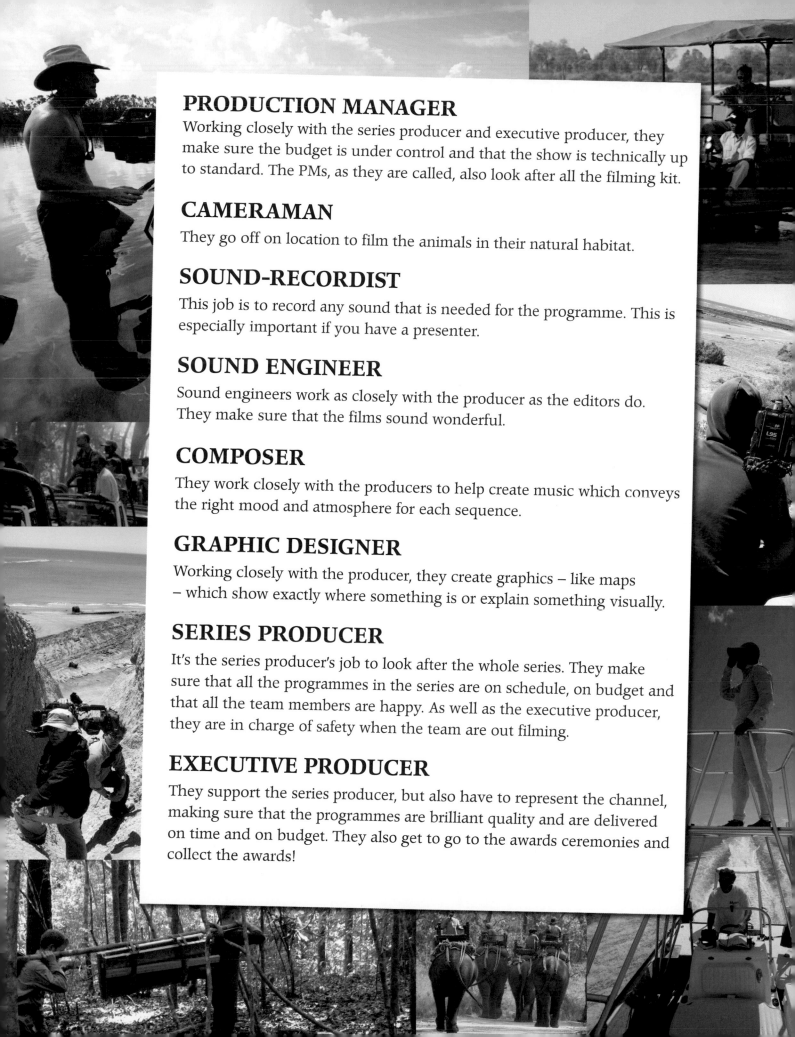

PRODUCTION MANAGER

Working closely with the series producer and executive producer, they make sure the budget is under control and that the show is technically up to standard. The PMs, as they are called, also look after all the filming kit.

CAMERAMAN

They go off on location to film the animals in their natural habitat.

SOUND-RECORDIST

This job is to record any sound that is needed for the programme. This is especially important if you have a presenter.

SOUND ENGINEER

Sound engineers work as closely with the producer as the editors do. They make sure that the films sound wonderful.

COMPOSER

They work closely with the producers to help create music which conveys the right mood and atmosphere for each sequence.

GRAPHIC DESIGNER

Working closely with the producer, they create graphics – like maps – which show exactly where something is or explain something visually.

SERIES PRODUCER

It's the series producer's job to look after the whole series. They make sure that all the programmes in the series are on schedule, on budget and that all the team members are happy. As well as the executive producer, they are in charge of safety when the team are out filming.

EXECUTIVE PRODUCER

They support the series producer, but also have to represent the channel, making sure that the programmes are brilliant quality and are delivered on time and on budget. They also get to go to the awards ceremonies and collect the awards!

EQUIPMENT

HIGH-SPEED CAMERAS

You might think that high-speed cameras make everything look fast, but they actually make everything look slow. The camera takes lots of pictures as an animal moves – it captures every movement they make. When the film is slowed down, we see exactly how the animal moves. A movement that happened in a second will now look like it took forty seconds.

TIMELAPSE CAMERAS

These are the exact opposite of high-speed cameras. They take single pictures of the same scene over a set amount of time. When these pictures are combined, it looks like a lot of time has passed very quickly. Timelapse cameras are used to film things that take a long time to happen, like the seasons changing or a flower opening.

HD camera

HIGH-DEFINITION CAMERAS

High-definition (or HD) cameras are an important piece of camera equipment. You can attach different lenses to these cameras which let you film things really close, really big or *really* far away. High-definition basically means these cameras see more when they record the pictures than the usual cameras.

MACRO HD CAMERAS

To film small things like ants or shrimp, you need a camera that is almost like a microscope so that the animals appear loads bigger.

CINEFLEX

These are cameras that are attached to moving vehicles like helicopters or jeeps – but they remain perfectly steady. This is because the camera is balanced on a gyroscope, which means it never moves up and down. They are expensive but amazing!

DOLLIES AND JIBS

Dollies are great fun. They are cameras fitted to things that allow them to move smoothly while you are filming – like a tripod on wheels or tracks, or a camera sliding down a zip wire. Jibs are small cranes that allow the camera to film up high and then down low in one smooth movement.

UNDERWATER HOUSING

To film underwater, you need a housing for your camera. This is a large watertight box that your camera fits inside. Although it keeps the camera dry, the box makes it tricky to film. It is a real specialist skill to learn how to use these cameras underwater.

underwater camera

TRIPODS

These are essential. To take good pictures, your camera needs to be rock steady, especially when you're filming wildlife – and tripods help you do this. Big sturdy tripods mean that the pictures are brilliant, but they are really heavy to carry on location. The amazing pictures you get make it all worthwhile though.

INFRARED CAMERAS

Used at night, they reveal the world when everything gets dark. You still need lights though – special ones that the animals can't see but the camera can.

All these cameras and pieces of equipment allow the LIFE team to film nature from different angles and different speeds, helping you see life from new and exciting perspectives. It also helps you to understand how an animal or plant might see the world around us.

23

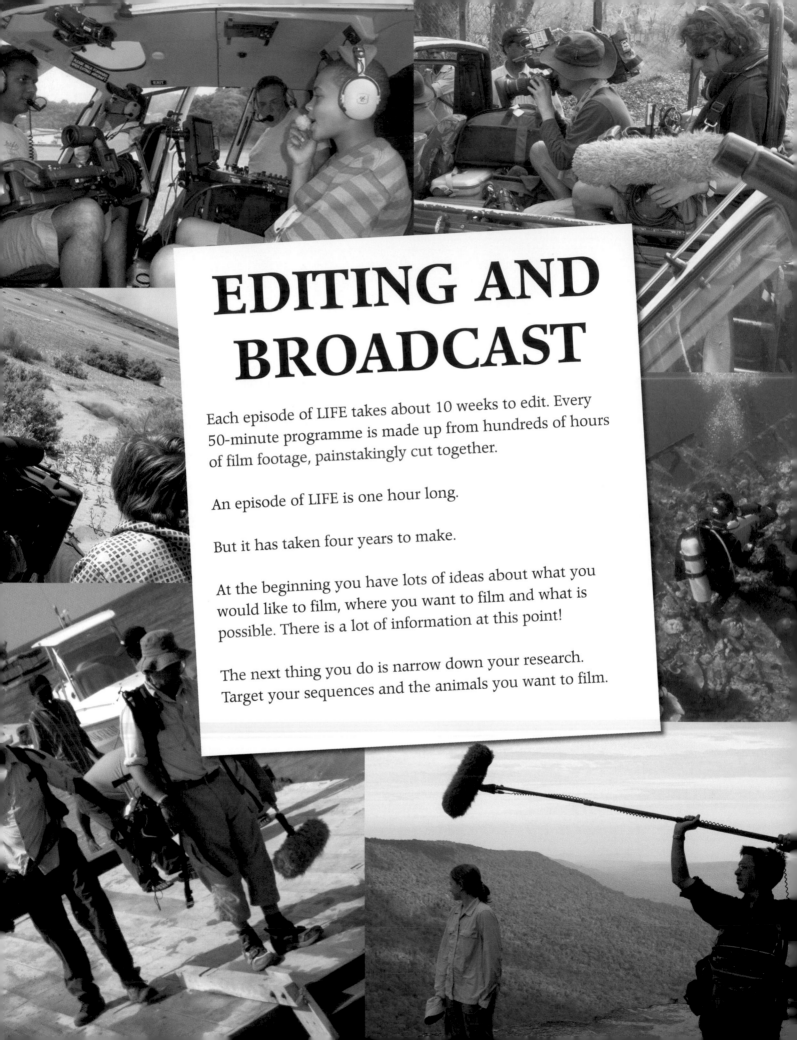

EDITING AND BROADCAST

Each episode of LIFE takes about 10 weeks to edit. Every 50-minute programme is made up from hundreds of hours of film footage, painstakingly cut together.

An episode of LIFE is one hour long.

But it has taken four years to make.

At the beginning you have lots of ideas about what you would like to film, where you want to film and what is possible. There is a lot of information at this point!

The next thing you do is narrow down your research. Target your sequences and the animals you want to film.

Then you go out filming, although not everything you want to film works. Animals don't always do what they are told – they haven't read the script!

In the edit you stick together the sequences that you have been able to film, but because not everything works, you will always have filmed more than you need. So only some of the sequences that you have filmed make it into the final programme.

With just a few tweaks, some music and sound, you have your finished programme – one in a series of ten. And that is what gets shown on television!

For each 50-minute episode of TV that you watch, four years' work was needed to make it.

So from 2,102,400 minutes of work you get to watch 50 minutes of television!

RING-TAILED LEMURS

TOP SECRET

MISSION:
Ring-tailed lemurs

AGENT:
Billy

ALIAS:
Bill

FACT-FINDING

Billy went to Woburn Safari Park to ask Jake, one of the park keepers, what he knew about lemurs. He found out that ring-tailed lemurs are very territorial and can get into massive scraps – so they really do behave badly! It was just what the LIFE team were looking for.

The Facts

❀ Lemurs are only found on the island of Madagascar.

❀ There are nearly 100 known species and sub-species of lemur.

❀ Ring-tailed lemurs are the most sociable and live in large groups of up to 34.

❀ The young ride around on their mothers' backs.

❀ The largest lemur species are the indri. They can grow up to 90 centimetres tall and weigh up to 10kg.

❀ Mouse lemurs are the smallest species.

Woburn

mouse lemur

MISSION: IN UK – FIND OUT HOW LEMURS BEHAVE

FEEDING TIME

Billy got to feed the black and white ruffed lemurs that they keep at Woburn. Their fur is so soft but they did get a little carried away and spent most of the time climbing all over the LIFE cameraman!

WHAT TO LOOK FOR

❧ Ring-tailed lemurs are more terrestrial than other lemurs.

❧ When it's sunny they spend their time sunbathing.

❧ Female lemurs are dominant over male lemurs.

❧ An average group consists of 17 male and female lemurs, with one dominant female.

At the end of his day with Jake, Billy was told that he was going to go to Madagascar to find some lemurs in the wild with the BBC team filming LIFE! He couldn't believe it!

MISSION: IN MADAGASCAR – FIND SOME LEMURS BEHAVING BADLY

Boarding Pass

LONDON

NORTH AMERICA

ASIA

EUROPE

AFRICA

MADAGASCAR

SOUTH AMERICA

AUSTRALASIA

WHERE WE STAYED

Everyone stayed in their own bungalow. They each had a bathroom, although not with any hot water. It was very comfortable and a great place to visit. Tourists visit Berenty (a Wildlife Reserve in southern Madagascar) as it is the best place in the world to watch lemurs in their natural habitat.

Every night the generator switches off at ten o'clock. If you are out and about and you have forgotten your torch, then you have to use the light of the stars and the moon to guide you!

the bungalows

A BIT ABOUT BERENTY

Berenty is one of the quietest and most peaceful places on earth. It is home to six species of lemur. Three species are diurnal (which is a fancy way of saying they are awake during the day). The other three are nocturnal (which is the opposite of diurnal, they are only awake at night).

chameleon

The things that make Madagascar so special

❈ Lemurs – this is the only place in the world you can see lemurs in the wild.

❈ Madagascar is home to nearly 50% of all the species of chameleon in the world.

❈ Even though it is very close to Africa, it has no venomous snakes, no lions or leopards, no elephants or rhinos. The scariest creatures in Madagascar are probably the spiders and they can't hurt you at all! So if you get lost in the dark, you are quite safe from the wildlife.

❈ It has tropical rainforests, deserts, woods, beaches, cold mountains and hot grasslands – this place has everything.

Facts about Madagascar

❈ It's the world's fourth biggest island.

❈ Because it's so isolated, most of its mammals, half of its birds and most of its plants exist nowhere else on earth.

❈ The island is very exposed to tropical cyclones.

Greetings from . . .

MADAGASCAR

AS SOON AS WE ARRIVED IN BERENTY WE SAW . . .

Verreaux's sifakas – large, white lemurs that have brown patches on their foreheads.

Brown lemurs – these live in small groups and spend most of their time eating. They grunt at each other like piglets.

Verreaux's sifaka

brown lemur

ring-tailed lemurs

Ring-tailed lemurs – a troop walked past with their tails high in the air.

LIFE TEAM

The LIFE team were Rosie and Gavin. There are some 15 troops of lemurs that live at Berenty and each morning the LIFE team, with the help of two experts, would visit the troops to see what they were up to. If there was any sign of fighting, then the radios would burst into life and everyone would start shouting directions at each other.

FIGHT!

The lemurs that the LIFE team were filming lived on the other side of the reserve and one morning the lemurs had a massive fight. Billy got the call and with Hadj, one of the local guides and a supreme lemur expert, he headed out to see what was going on. Billy and Hadj didn't get too close. They didn't want to get in the way of the LIFE team as they had been waiting for a couple of weeks to film this behaviour!

BERENTY LEMURS

The ring-tailed lemurs at Berenty are habituated. This means they are not tame but they don't mind people. If you get too close, they give a bark and run off. If you sit down and don't pose a threat, then they tend to wander around you.

JOB DONE

Billy had done his job and got the LIFE team the story they wanted. And not only that – he had seen lemurs everywhere.

MISSION: COMPLETED!

KOMODO DRAGONS

LONDON ZOO

Izzy was invited to London Zoo to meet Dr Ian Stevens who looks after Raja, London Zoo's big male Komodo dragon. Komodo dragons are the largest lizards in the world and they are impossible to imagine until you see them in the flesh. Izzy asked Ian all about dragons – what she didn't know was that this information was going to be put to the test!

The Facts

❀ They have a deadly saliva which is full of bacteria. Once they have struck down their prey they wait for it to die from infection.

❀ Young dragons hatch from eggs and hide in trees for up to five years to escape the adult dragons.

❀ They live on the Indonesian islands of Komodo, Rinca and Padar.

❀ They live in open woodland, scrubby hillsides and dry river beds.

❀ They eat snakes, lizards, chickens, ducks, cats, dogs, wild pigs, water buffalo and deer.

❀ It's the only lizard species that hunts and kills prey much larger than itself.

Komodo Island

MISSION: IN UK – FIND OUT WHAT YOU HAVE TO LOOK FOR WHEN SEARCHING FOR KOMODO DRAGONS

LOOKING AFTER RAJA

Izzy helped to clean and feed Raja. He is quite sociable for a Komodo dragon – a bit like a big dog, as Izzy found out! She also helped with his target training. Every time he touched his target (a white ball on a stick) he was rewarded. This means it's much easier to work with him, and if he needs treatment the keepers can handle him safely. Ian told Izzy what to look out for when looking for a Komodo dragon in the wild.

At the end of her day with Ian, Izzy was told that she was going to go to Komodo to find some dragons in the wild with the BBC team filming LIFE! She was over the moon!

WHAT TO LOOK FOR

❀ TRAIL TRACKS
Dragons drag their tails when walking, so you always find lines drawn in the sand where a dragon has walked.

❀ FOOTPRINTS
They have sharp claws so leave footprints. Their prints look a little bit like someone has pushed the tips of 3 or 4 pencils into the ground.

❀ POO!
Their poo is white and hard. And often has animal bones in it.

Komodo dragons weigh up to 80kg.

Komodo dragons grow to over three metres long.

MISSION: IN KOMODO – FIND SOME DRAGONS!

Boarding Pass

LONDON

NORTH AMERICA

ASIA

EUROPE

AFRICA

INDONESIA

SOUTH AMERICA

AUSTRALASIA

WHERE WE STAYED

We slept on a boat. Each cabin had bunk-beds and its own little bathroom. One night we slept on deck underneath the stars, which was amazing but it did get chilly in the morning.

our boat!

Komodo – the Facts

❀ Komodo Island is 35km long and 15km wide.

❀ For most of the year Komodo is dry and hot.

❀ Komodo National Park was set up in 1980 and was declared a World Heritage Site by UNESCO in 1986.

❀ Komodo National Park is lots of islands, including Komodo, Rinca and Padar.

Greetings from KOMODO

There are about 5,000 dragons in Indonesia. They all live on Komodo, Rinca and Padar.

A BIT ABOUT KOMODO

Komodo is a marine wildlife reserve with high mountains and deep valleys full of trees and bushes. It's hot. Really, really hot! So most of the filming was done early in the morning before the sun was high in the sky, or in the cool of the evening. In our spare time we snorkelled around the reefs, which are some of the best in the world! One morning we saw dolphins but they were quite far away. And we fished, although we never caught a single thing.

The LIFE team had heard that dragons had been spotted, so we met up with our guide to investigate . . .

Finding the dragons – Ready to go!

Remember what to look for:-

• The lines from their tails in the sand
• Their footprints
• Their poo

our guide

OUR GUIDE

The guide was armed with a long forked stick to protect us. No guns, no knives – just a stick! If a dragon gets too close, they poke and prod it until the dragon goes in the direction they want it to. It doesn't always work, but dragons rarely if ever attack if they are out in the open. It's the dragon you don't see that you have to be worried about.

Dragons are predators and attack by ambush. They have even been known to attack humans.

BABY DRAGON

We saw a baby dragon climbing a tree. They do this to keep out of the way of big dragons, which given the chance will eat them. If the youngsters were nervous, this was a good sign as it meant that there were adults nearby.

Our first discoveries

❀ Footprints and tail prints.

❀ Poo and animal bones.

❀ A cockatoo.

❀ A baby dragon.

When you see a dragon for the first time, it doesn't seem real. A living breathing wild Komodo dragon is massive. It's what looking at a dinosaur must have felt like.

36

Suddenly we realized that we weren't alone. Three Komodo dragons were coming straight at us and the smallest was easily 2.5 metres long! Thankfully it was early evening and the dragons were tired, having been on the beach all day looking for food. They wanted to relax, rest and wait for the morning sun, so it could warm their bodies enough for the eternal search for food to continue.

Incredibly, Komodo dragons have lived on these islands for thousands of years.

MISSION: COMPLETED!

POLAR BEARS

THE SNOWDOME!

Lou knew her mission was going to be a chilly one when she turned up for filming at the SnowDome in Tamworth. She met up with Rosie Stancer, one of the world's top polar explorers. Rosie knows a thing or two about surviving sub-zero temperatures and was ready with some top tips.

How to survive in Arctic temperatures

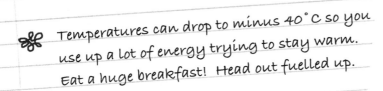

❀ Temperatures can drop to minus 40°C so you use up a lot of energy trying to stay warm. Eat a huge breakfast! Head out fuelled up.

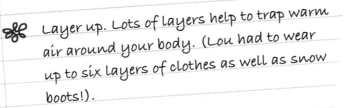

❀ Layer up. Lots of layers help to trap warm air around your body. (Lou had to wear up to six layers of clothes as well as snow boots!).

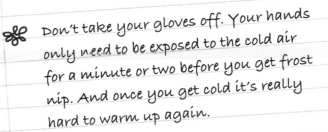

❀ Don't take your gloves off. Your hands only need to be exposed to the cold air for a minute or two before you get frost nip. And once you get cold it's really hard to warm up again.

❀ Avoid touching any metal on the camera with your bare hands. Your skin could freeze to it – ouch!

Lou and crew, layered up!

COLD CONDITIONS

Working in the extreme cold can become a matter of life or death. Rosie showed Lou how to stop frostbite when the temperatures fall. Lou was able to find out what kind of clothes she should wear in the Arctic, and she found out that eating lots of food is the key to surviving.

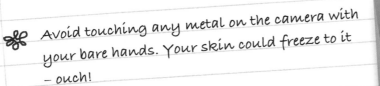

MISSION: IN UK – FIND OUT HOW TO COPE WITH FILMING WILDLIFE IN FREEZING TEMPERATURES

HYPOTHERMIA – WHAT IS IT?

Hypothermia happens when your body temperature falls below 35°C. Getting really cold and wet for a long period of time can bring it on. You can tell if somebody is hypothermic when they are shivering and their skin goes cold and pale. People with hypothermia can become confused, stumble around and eventually fall unconscious. It can be fatal.

What to look for

❀ Polar bears live in the Arctic Circle where temperatures get as low as minus 40°C.

❀ They are armed with thick fur, up to 15cm long, to keep them warm.

❀ Polar bears have huge claws, perfect for gripping seals and keeping a firm hold on the ice.

❀ These bears can run at speeds of about 40 kmph for short bursts.

❀ Polar bears are great swimmers with great big paddle-like feet to help them move through the water.

❀ Their favourite food is seals.

DON'T FREEZE!

Filming wildlife often requires sitting still for a long time, but you need to jump up and down every now and then so you don't freeze. Lou even found out how to go to the loo in the snow without getting frostbite.

Lou also found out how to use a bear flare to keep any hungry polar bears at bay. As if the huge bang from the flare wasn't enough, Lou then got the shock of finding out that she would be heading to the Arctic herself – on a mission to film polar bears!

MISSION: IN THE ARCTIC – FIND SOME POLAR BEARS!

Boarding Pass

KAKTOVIK

LONDON

NORTH AMERICA

EUROPE

AFRICA

ASIA

GETTING THERE

Squeezing into a very small plane to travel over one of the world's biggest wildernesses was a bit scary. As you fly over snow-topped peaks it looks like there is nothing below – and there isn't. There are no roads, no landing strips, no lights, nothing.

our plane!

WHERE WE STAYED

When we arrived at our base in the Arctic village of Kaktovik, it was like landing on the moon. Only when we were clear of the airstrip did the tiny cluster of ramshackle houses appear out of the rubble and ice.

The guest house was made from containers that carry cargo on ships. They were joined up to make rooms. It was weird but really cosy. With the heating on full blast we were protected from the 128kmph winds outside.

our cosy room!

A BIT ABOUT KAKTOVIK

Kaktovik is one of the most northerly points of the USA. It's in Alaska and has a population of around 300 people.

ALASKA

THE MISSION

Lou's mission was to find out from cameraman Doug Allan how to film polar bears. He's probably filmed more polar bears than anyone else in the world and is a real expert on their behaviour. Doug's job is a risky one and he needs an assistant to watch his back. Polar bears can be very dangerous creatures. When Doug is trying to get great shots of the bears, most of his attention is focused down the lens of the camera. On the ice, polar bears can appear out of nowhere, so Doug told Lou to keep looking around to check that none crept up or caught them unawares.

What to watch out for when filming bears

❀ Large tracks in the snow.

❀ Leftovers. Any signs of a bear having had a snack, like blood or bones.

❀ Bears appearing out of nowhere. Often their white bodies are camouflaged against the snow as they creep up on you.

❀ If a bear does approach, make sure you can get into the back-up vehicle without anything blocking your way.

❀ Is the ice sheet strong enough to hold your weight? Fall through it into the icy sea and you are unlikely to survive for more than a few minutes.

Lou's kit list

- ✔ Thermal leggings
- ✔ Woolly tights
- ✔ Thermal vest
- ✔ Thermal long-sleeved top layer
- ✔ Woolly jumper / thin fleece layer
- ✔ Thick fleece layer
- ✔ Down jacket
- ✔ Neoprene face mask
- ✔ Neck warmer
- ✔ Scarf
- ✔ Warm woolly hat
- ✔ Thin silk gloves
- ✔ Thick mittens
- ✔ Hand warmers
- ✔ Thin socks
- ✔ Thick ski socks
- ✔ Snow boots
- ✔ Sleeping bag
- ✔ Hot water bottle
- ✔ 2 flasks of hot chocolate
- ✔ Lots of high-energy snacks
- ✔ Walkie-talkie to contact base
- ✔ Binoculars
- ✔ Pepper spray
- ✔ Bear flare

ARCTIC CONDITIONS

When the Arctic sea freezes it is called sea ice. First the sea becomes like an icy porridge, and then it gets very thick until it melts again. Polar bears have to make the most of the sea freezing up as it gives them more space in which to look for food. Climate change is making it harder for bears to hunt on the ice as it is melting faster.

View from the pick-up

on the edge of the sea ice

LOOKING FOR BEARS

Where the ice was thick enough, we were able to drive around on it to look for bears. Sometimes they would be way off in the distance. If the sky was cloudy white, it was very hard to see where the sky stopped and the snow began – conditions that made it even harder to see a bear.

hunting for food

Bears and humans

❋ Most bears are scared of humans but will take the risk especially when there is food involved.

❋ Kaktovik is a town with some Inuit people living there.

❋ They are used to having the bears as neighbours, but have to be really careful about leaving any food outside.

❋ Sometimes the bears come into town and the children aren't able to walk to school in case they meet a hungry bear!

Sometimes large males will kill and eat a young bear.

SEEING BEARS

During filming, Doug and Lou saw a female bear with her two young cubs. The first time they saw them, they were all cuddled up together on the ice which made them really hard to see but they were really cute. Later on, they saw them playing together. Even though the cubs were only about a year old, they got really feisty while they were playing. They had huge big paws and kept leaping around on the ice.

SCARY SITUATION

One day during filming, we saw a big male bear chase away a female bear with her cubs. It was amazing to see this huge creature up close. Lou was transfixed, but then she remembered to keep looking for any other bears that might show up. She looked around just in time to see another big male approach. Quickly she let Doug know the situation. They got in the pick-up just before the second bear got too close. The bear came right up to the vehicle. It was a pretty scary moment – we wanted to get close to the bears so that we could film, but not that close!

MISSION: COMPLETED!

THE SHOAL

TOP SECRET

MISSION:
The shoal

AGENT:
Sam

ALIAS:
Sammy

FILMING UNDERWATER

Sam was taken to West Wales to learn all about filming underwater. The biggest difficulty is finding things in the first place. You could swim around and hope you see something, but you're only able to cover a very small distance and you would get tired very quickly. The best thing to do is watch the water from above and look out for clues that let you know something is happening below. The first part of Sam's mission was to pick up the tricks of watching waves.

The tricks of watching water

✿ Get high, as high as you can, this gives you the best view of the most water.

✿ Use binoculars or a scope.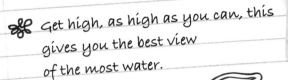

✿ Look out for:
  • birds flying about
  • Fins and water spouts (this means there are whales or dolphins swimming nearby)

When you see these, you know you've found a shoal of fish.

seagulls overhead!

LOOKING FOR DOLPHINS

In November, New Quay in West Wales is the most likely place to see dolphins in the UK. Sam turned up wrapped in thermals, waterproofs and smiles.

He met up with dolphin expert Mark Cawardine and Steve Hartley, the boat skipper and head of the dolphin research team.

The best days for dolphin and whale watching are flat calm days, when the air is clear and sunny. Then you can see for miles. The day in New Quay was rainy, choppy and cloudy, so none of us were that surprised we didn't see anything. And of course Sam had no idea that this was just the start of things.

Sam got a real shock when he found out that he was to use his new-found knowledge and fly to South America where the LIFE team were waiting for his help.

MISSION: IN PATAGONIA – HELP FIND A HUGE SHOAL OF FISH FOR THE LIFE TEAM

LONDON

NORTH AMERICA

EUROPE

ASIA

SOUTH AMERICA

PATAGONIA

Boarding Pass

WHERE WE STAYED

We stayed in Puerto Piramides, a small village on the southern tip of the Peninsula Valdes. It's a famous destination for whale watching and hunting anchovy shoals. Peninsula Valdes, halfway down the coast of Argentina, is a huge nature reserve on a small spit of land that sticks out into the ocean.

A BIT ABOUT PATAGONIA

Patagonia takes up most of southern Argentina and southern Chile. It stretches from the glaciers of the Andes mountains to the Atlantic coast, where southern right whales gather to breed. It has a huge elephant seal colony and the world's largest Magellanic penguin colony. It's a nature lover's dream!

penguin colony

Magellanic penguin

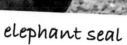
elephant seal

southern right whale

The other animals that live in the area

❀ Guanacos – are like llamas but thinner and more sophisticated.

❀ Penguins – these are Magellanic penguins and they love eating anchovies.

❀ Elephant seals – so called because the males have huge noses.

❀ Southern right whales – like to give birth in these waters. You will often see mothers with their calves swimming off the shore.

BAD WEATHER

Good weather for this mission was essential. If conditions were bad, then it would be impossible to launch any boats. And if you were lucky enough to sail out and the weather turned bad, you would have to return straight away so you wouldn't get stranded at sea. This was frustrating for the LIFE team, but gave Sam the opportunity to have a look around.

Facts about the shoal

❀ Anchovies are small silvery fish which are usually no longer than your finger. →

❀ They live in such vast numbers that a shoal can number hundreds of thousands of little fish. Seeing them swim is one of nature's most amazing spectacles.

❀ These shoals provide food for other fish, penguins, dolphins, sharks, sea lions and even whales!

❀ The shoal protects itself by dancing. The fish shimmer and flash as they move together. This behaviour is believed to confuse predators.

Anchovy

The LIFE team wanted to film these little fish as they performed their synchronized swimming dance.

47

SPOTTING A SHOAL

Sam's second half of his mission was to help spot a shoal for the LIFE team. The plan was simple. The team would go out in a boat while Sam went up onto cliffs above the bay to keep an eye out. Sam would contact the team by radio or mobile phone if he spotted any activity.

watching . . .

and waiting . . .

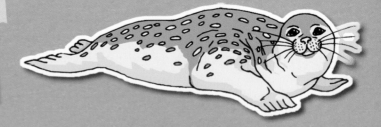

the Cessna!

TAKE TO THE SKIES

After days of searching, they still couldn't find anything. Sam took a flight in a Cessna, which is a small plane, to get a bird's-eye view of the whole bay. You can only stay in the air for a few hours though, and Sam still had no luck. Although he did see a whale – which was amazing.

When we got back, the LIFE team were on the beach. They had just got back from filming a shoal. Success! Sam celebrated as if he had scored the World Cup winner.

MISSION: COMPLETED!

GIBBONS

MISSION:
Gibbons

AGENT:
Bryony

ALIAS:
Bry

TESTING EQUIPMENT

Bryony met up with Tim and Pam Fogg to find out all about the specialist equipment needed to film high up in the treetops. Tim and Pam advise camera crews on how to safely use ropes to climb trees. They were testing out a specially built filming platform that was going to be used on a LIFE filming trip to the rainforest. Bryony's job was to help test the platform and make sure it would be solid enough for use.

How to film at heights

❀ Wear comfy clothes, but make sure they're not too baggy. They could get caught in the ropes.

❀ A hard hat stops you banging your head and protects you from things falling.

❀ Climbing a tall tree is hard work, so pace yourself and drink lots beforehand.

❀ Avoid rustling leaves and snapping branches where possible. This will scare the wildlife as you climb.

❀ Make sure your filming equipment is secured so that it doesn't fall on anybody below.

❀ Be prepared to spend all day up in the trees – you need food, water and, possibly, something to pee into!

❀ A platform is essential; dangling in a harness is uncomfortable, and dangerous after a little while.

The best time to see the gibbons was as soon as the sun rose so the crew would get to the trees in darkness, ready to begin filming at first light.

CLIMBING THE TREES

Climbing high up in the forest canopy is only dangerous if you fall. With the correct safety equipment and ropes, filming at these great heights is pretty secure.

MISSION: IN UK – FIND OUT HOW TO FILM GIBBONS HIGH UP IN THE RAINFOREST CANOPY

FILMING GIBBONS

Gibbons are very tricky to film. They wake up before sunrise and then they move off quickly through the canopy. You have to stay on their trail if you are going to film them. Gibbons move fast through the forest, so you need to be prepared to do a fair bit of jogging over steep and uneven ground.

THE RAINFOREST

The temperature in the rainforest is hot and humid. There are lots of insects, but you soon get used to them buzzing around. As long as you cover up with the right clothes and use repellent, you shouldn't get bitten.

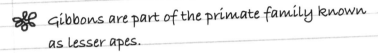

Gibbons - the Facts

❀ Gibbons are part of the primate family known as lesser apes.

❀ They are endangered.

❀ Gibbons live high up in the rainforest canopy and rarely come down to ground level.

❀ They inhabit many parts of South East Asia.

❀ They have thick fur to protect them from the heavy monsoon rains.

❀ They live in families or troops.

❀ 50% of their diet is fruit.

❀ With their long arms they can jump gaps in the trees of almost 10 metres.

❀ Some gibbons can live as long as 44 years.

At the top, Tim revealed that Bryony would be going with the platform to Thailand to climb trees as tall as 20 metres! Hopefully she would also get to see gibbons in the wild.

MISSION: IN THAILAND – FIND OUT ABOUT GIBBONS AND FILM THEM IN THE RAINFOREST

Boarding Pass

MISSION: IN THAILAND – FIND OUT ABOUT GIBBONS AND FILM THEM IN THE RAINFOREST

NORTH AMERICA

LONDON

EUROPE

ASIA

AFRICA

THAILAND

A BIT ABOUT BANGKOK

First we stopped in Bangkok. It's the capital of Thailand and very hot and noisy. You are swallowed up in the traffic, heat and different smells. About nine million people live here, which is why it is so busy.

Bryony hadn't been anywhere this hot before. It took her a few days to get used to the bustle and soaring temperatures. However, there are places to chill out in Bangkok. There are plenty of very ornate Buddhist temples where you can get away from the heat and noise. Bryony whizzed around in a tuk-tuk, one of the best ways to see the sights!

WHERE WE STAYED

We eventually headed out of Bangkok and into the countryside to Khao Yai National Park. Things were a lot quieter here. Lots of people farm the land outside of the city and everyone is the friendliest they can be. It's a long drive from Bangkok to where the gibbons live but there are lots of cool things to see on the way. Inside the park we saw a huge python, thousands of bats, macaques and sambar deer!

getting around

52

MISSION GIBBON

The main reason for Bryony's trip was to help the LIFE team track down and film the gibbons. The first task was to find out where in the huge rainforest they were hanging out. To get their exact position, Bryony headed out with a researcher called Uwe. She was an expert at trailing the gibbons. They spent several sweltering hours racing around the forest, hot on the trail of these primates. It was important to radio any new sightings back to the rest of the LIFE team.

How to successfully track gibbons

❀ Keep an eye out for gibbon poo.

❀ Smell.

❀ Lots of rustling above, followed by movement in the trees.

❀ Any falling fruit – so mind your head.

❀ Be prepared to get a crick in the neck.

❀ Be really quiet!

SETTING UP

Once we knew that the gibbons were going to stay put in one place, it was time to get the special platform up so that it could be used as a base from which to film.

Camerawoman Justine Evans is an experienced climber who is nuts about big trees. She's filmed gibbons many times before and spends a lot of time up high. Bryony set about the challenge of joining her over 20 metres up the tree – no easy feat.

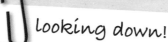
Justine

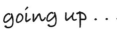
going up . . .

looking down!

Bryony's kit list for filming in the rainforest

☑ Water bottle containing at least 2 litres of water
☑ Walkie-talkie to contact base for sightings and in an emergency
☑ Binoculars
☑ Glucose tablets
☑ Wide-brimmed hat
☑ Leech socks
☑ Sturdy boots
☑ Lightweight fleece
☑ Lightweight shirt with long sleeves and collar
☑ Wet wipes
☑ Climbing harness
☑ Hard hat
☑ Various climbing gear
☑ Mosquito repellent

RAINFOREST CONDITIONS

Life in the rainforest tends to be hot and sticky. Warm temperatures mix with the heavy rains, which means it gets very humid. Because the forest can be so thick, it's often really dark down at ground level so to get around you have to sometimes cut a trail through the bushes. The trees grow so well in the forest that it makes it difficult to see a lot of the animals living there. When you are looking for gibbons you might only get little glimpses of them above.

Dense forest means it's also harder to see snakes and elephants, which you definitely want to avoid!

WILDLIFE FRIENDS FOUNDATION – THAILAND

Bryony visited the Gibbon Rehabilitation Centre run by the Wildlife Friends Foundation – Thailand. Here she met many young gibbons separated from their mothers through hunting and the pet trade. At the sanctuary they try to let the gibbons live in as natural an environment as possible before releasing them back into the wild.

GIBBONS AT RISK

More and more rainforests are being cleared for agriculture, displacing gibbon families and destroying their homes. When the forests get cut down, many gibbon families get split up. Hunters will also seek out young and baby gibbons that end up in the pet trade. This means they will eventually be sold in markets or used as tourist attractions.

SINGING AND DANCING GIBBONS

Seeing gibbons in the trees is like watching a high-wire ballet. They swing from branch to branch as if it's the easiest thing in the world. Using their arms like this to get about is called 'brachiation'. Their hands and feet are designed to hook and grip onto the branches as they move around.

But gibbons don't just dance through the trees – they also call to each other with a loud musical song. Listening to the gibbons' chorus is one way to find out where they are. First of all, a male and female will start a duet which builds up to a massive hooting sound through the forest. These operatics get louder and louder until it is deafening!

THE BIG CLIMB

After days of tracking the gibbons, top camerawoman Justine was getting close. One of the researchers had seen the gibbons and they were headed towards her. Bryony waited until Justine gave her the thumbs up to join her in the tree. It was crucial that the noise from Bryony climbing didn't scare the gibbons off. If the gibbons disappeared, it might be days before they'd be found again.

After sitting at the bottom of the tree for two hours, Bryony got the signal. Climbing up the ropes was exhausting and took nearly half an hour in searing heat. She had only just got her breath back when the family of gibbons swung through the treetops into the clearing in front of them. Like a flash Justine swung the camera round on them and they quietly watched while these acrobatic apes danced and sang before them.

MISSION: COMPLETED!

FRIGATE BIRDS

MISSION:
Frigate birds

AGENT:
Gregory

ALIAS:
Greg

Different Cameras

✿ A standard camera can be hand-held or put on a tripod.

✿ One chip or three chip cameras are small cameras that need to be attached to a recorder, a hard drive or a tape deck.

✿ Thermal cameras see and film heat (see Garter snakes).

✿ Borescope cameras are long narrow cameras that you can push into small holes and other tight gaps.

✿ Mounted cameras or cineflex are special cameras that can be mounted on boats, cars even helicopters.

BIRD'S-EYE VIEW!

Greg was going to see how different kinds of cameras can be used to help film some natural history sequences about bird behaviour. He went down to the south coast to meet up with Geoff Bell, who specializes in fitting small cameras to remote control helicopters and vehicles. Any camera fitted onto a helicopter costs a lot of money, so you have to be very careful with it, but what you get is a different view of the world around you. Using small cameras lets us see the world from all sorts of different angles.

cineflex camera . . .

. . . on helicopter

standard camera

MISSION: IN UK — FIND OUT HOW YOU FILM AERIAL IMAGES

FILMING!

When filming an episode completely on birds, the LIFE team had to think about how to film from the point of view of the animal. How do you get a bird's-eye view? The team knew they would have to get into the air. They had two options; either the cameraman and his camera could fly in a helicopter or an aeroplane, or the camera could fly attached to a helicopter.

inside the helicopter

the crew

FLYING THE HELICOPTER

Geoff let Greg fly the helicopter outside. The film looks like a bird swooping over the countryside. This isn't exactly what birds see but it gives you a good idea. Keeping the camera steady is really tricky but Greg got the hang of it.

He did it so well that Geoff revealed to Greg the next phase of his mission . . .

He was going to fly in a helicopter on the island of Tobago, which is in the Caribbean.

Greg at the controls

MISSION IN TOBAGO – HELP FILM FRIGATE BIRDS, THE PIRATES OF THE SKIES, WITH THE LIFE TEAM

Boarding Pass

ISLAND STATS

- Closest island to South America
- Length – 42km
- Width – 11km
- Weather – mainly hot and sunny (apart from in hurricane season!)

NORTH AMERICA

LONDON

ASIA

EUROPE

TOBAGO

AFRICA

ABOUT TOBAGO

Tobago is one of the last islands in the chain that is known as the Caribbean. This island chain was formed by volcanic activity millions of years ago, and many of the islands still have active volcanoes. In 1997 the volcano on Montserrat erupted and lots of people had to evacuate their homes.

The other animals that live on Tobago

❀ Caiman crocodiles.

❀ Colourful crabs.

❀ Howler monkeys – have the loudest calls of any monkey.

❀ The quenk – which is a white-collared peccary, a type of small pig.

❀ Loads of birds! Seven different kinds of hummingbird as well as tropic birds and of course, the frigate birds.

BATTLE OF THE BIRDS

Frigate birds are large black birds with forked tails and long beaks. They look a lot like pterodactyls which flew the skies during the age of the dinosaurs. The males have large throat sacs that are bright red. Frigate birds are also known as the Pirates of the Skies. And as they live in the Caribbean, they really are the Pirates of the Caribbean!

male frigate bird

tropic bird

Tropic birds also live here. They are all white with a black eyebrow, a bright red beak and a very long thin white tail. They are excellent fishers. They nest on an island called Little Tobago. They are relatively tame and you can walk quite close to them. No people live on Little Tobago so they are not disturbed.

But . . . every day the tropic birds have to leave their nests to go fishing. And when they return, the frigate birds are waiting for them!

Facts about filming in the air

- ❁ Helicopters and small aeroplanes are used for filming in the air.

- ❁ Helicopters are easier to move around.

- ❁ Cameras fixed onto the helicopter are the best.

- ❁ You can change the picture using the remote control inside the cockpit.

birdwatching

MISSION IN TOBAGO – HELP FILM FRIGATE BIRDS, THE PIRATES OF THE SKIES, WITH THE LIFE TEAM

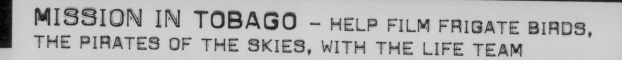

MISSION IN TOBAGO – HELP FILM FRIGATE BIRDS, THE PIRATES OF THE SKIES, WITH THE LIFE TEAM

WHAT HAPPENED?

Frigate birds are not just called pirates for fun. They lie in wait for tropic birds to return to their nests after a successful fishing trip; and then the frigate birds strike! They swoop down and grab the tropic birds by their tails in an attempt to scare them so much that they drop their fish. Next, with acrobatics worthy of a fighter pilot, the frigate birds let go of the tropic birds' tails and swoop down to steal their treasure in mid-air. Their mission is complete and their meal snatched!

Then the poor tropic birds have to start fishing all over again, hoping that those sneaky frigate birds will be full up by the time they return.

the 'pirates'!

tropic bird

frigate bird

60

THE PERFECT SHOT

Greg went with Simon Werry, who operated the camera that is fixed to the helicopter, to film some aerial shots. They wanted to film the island in the same way that the frigate birds would see it as they closed in on the fish-full tropic birds.

Using advanced technology allows us to see the world like the animals themselves see it. This technology is getting better and better. With the shot in the bag, Greg and Simon returned back to base, successful! And the frigate birds continued with their piracy.

Welcome to TOBAGO

After several fly-bys, the boys filmed a brilliant sequence that might very well make the final programme

MISSION: COMPLETED!

BENGAL TIGERS

LISTEN UP!

Scarlet was invited to Longleat Safari Park to meet up with Andrew Yarme. Andrew is a sound-recordist. Although most cameras have microphones attached, the sound they record is not good enough for film and this is where a sound-recordist comes in handy. They record the close-up sounds that the camera's microphone misses, and also the everyday sounds of the forest, desert, ice floe or swamp. The first part of Scarlet's mission was to see if she could record the sound of lions and tigers feeding.

The kit

❀ The microphone is what 'hears' the sound.

❀ The 'fluffy' is the fluffy cover on the mircrophone! It reduces the effect of wind when you are recording.

❀ The microphone is plugged into the equalizer. This balances the sound, stopping it from being too quiet or too loud.

❀ The equalizer is plugged into the recorder. This saves the sound which will be used later when you are putting the film together.

❀ Your headphones – you must wear them all the time. Anything you can hear in them is also being recorded, this includes people talking, aeroplanes, cars and mobile phones. You don't want any of this noise in your final film.

ready for action!

MISSION: IN UK – FIND OUT HOW ALL THE AMAZING SOUND IS RECORDED FOR A WILDLIFE SERIES LIKE LIFE

How animals use sound

❀ To talk to each other in a group. Lemurs grunt to let the others know they are near.

❀ To warn intruders they've wandered into their territory. Gibbons sing to declare that this is their patch.

❀ To find a mate. Lots of birds sing to show off to possible mates.

❀ To alert others that there is danger.

SOUNDS LIKE

One of the most important jobs a sound-recordist does is to capture the sounds animals use to talk to each other, like specific bird or animal calls.

GETTING UP CLOSE TO A BIG CAT!

Scarlet and Andrew sat inside a large metal cage which was strapped to the back of a truck and driven into the big cat enclosure. The keepers threw in the big cats' food. With her headphones on, Scarlet could hear the cats snarling, scrabbling, chomping and chewing. Because big cats are carnivores, they have teeth big enough to crunch bones! It is really loud, and even louder with a microphone and headphones on – it makes everything sound closer than it really is!

Andrew was really happy with Scarlet's work, so much so she was going to help him on his next assignment. But that meant going to India to see Bengal tigers in the wild!

MISSION IN INDIA – FIND AND RECORD THE NATURAL SOUND OF AN INDIAN TIGER FOREST

brilliant market!

hustle and bustle

SOME OF THE SIGHTS

We went to this market, it was completely amazing! There were nice, tasty smells followed by really awful ones! There was so much to look at and so many colours. The traffic in India was terrifying. Everyone was driving so fast, but no one ever seemed to crash into one another. Every so often you would see a cow walking down the middle of the street, and because cows are sacred you just had to sit and wait until the cow decided to get out of the way! We also visited the Taj Mahal. This beautiful building is made entirely out of white marble, took 22 years to create and was built in memory of a Muslim emperor's wife.

A BIT ABOUT BANDHAVGARH

In olden days, this beautiful region used to be a hunting ground. Shooting tigers used to be considered a sport, but soon the number of tigers in the wild began to drop dramatically. The Indian authorities decided to ban hunting and now the population of tigers is slowly beginning to increase.

This park is a wildlife paradise and the best place to see tigers in the wild!

When you enter the forest for the first time and stop and listen, you realize that there are a lot of different noises out there – some strange and funny, some familiar but from unusual animals.

Animal calls you might hear in the forest

❀ Chital deer bark like small dogs – it's really strange to hear.

❀ Hanuman langurs (a type of monkey) have a call like someone clearing their throat really loudly.

❀ Elephants trumpet, but you are more likely to hear them crashing through the vegetation.

❀ Peacocks live in these forests and have a harsh screeching call.

Facts about tigers

❀ Tigers are the biggest members of the cat family.

❀ Male Bengal tigers can reach up to 3 metres in length, females up to 2.7 metres.

❀ It is estimated that there are only about 3,000 Bengal tigers left in the wild.

❀ There are several good places in India to see tigers, Bandhavgarh is one of the best.

Scarlet and the crew

65

filming in the forest

WHAT HAPPENED?

We wanted to record the sounds of the forest, including the other animals, as if an intruder had wandered into their territory. We used a leopard puppet to demonstrate the kinds of calls that you could expect to hear. It was so convincing that all the animals called out as if it was a real leopard. Once the puppet had been put away all the animals settled down again and carried on as normal.

The forest was really hot and the team constantly had to drink water to make sure they didn't become dehydrated.

really peaceful . . . and really loud!

RECORDING THE SOUND

Scarlet helped Andrew record the sound of the forest; it was really peaceful, but also really loud.

elephant ride

HOW IT'S DONE

When you watch a wildlife film, all the sound you hear is put on afterwards. It means that the cameraman can capture the best images and the sound-recordist can capture the best sound. It is a specialist skill and the end result creates the best and most perfect atmosphere. So when you see a tiger walking in the forest, you also hear the forest as it really sounds.

Bengal tiger

MISSION: COMPLETED!

GARTER SNAKES

RAF

Matt was taken to a secret location in the south of England to hook up with the Royal Air Force. The RAF use thermal imaging cameras on search and rescue missions to help them find people lost at sea or on hillsides. The RAF are on 24-hour standby across the UK, and to make sure they are ready and prepared, they go on lots of training missions. Matt was joining them on one of these missions to see the thermal camera in action.

The Facts

❋ Thermal imaging cameras work in the same way as normal video cameras – except they use infrared radiation instead of light. Because of this they can also be used in the dark!

❋ On a thermal camera, the hottest part of the picture shows up white, then red; then orange, blue and green are the cooler parts.

❋ Some animals, like rattlesnakes, see objects using heat, just like these cameras.

❋ In the past, thermal cameras could only take still images, like photographs. Now, thermal cameras allow us to take moving pictures too.

at the airfield

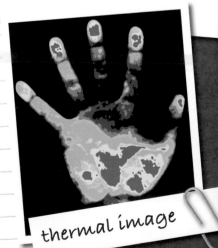

thermal image

MISSION: IN UK – TEST OUT THERMAL IMAGING CAMERA!

Sea King helicopter

SEA KING STATS

Sea Kings weigh more than two elephants. They can fly for hours without having to refuel and have a top speed of 230kmph! And they can fly in almost any weather conditions – making them perfect for search and rescue.

THERMAL IMAGING

Matt was dressed in an RAF jumpsuit, and then with the pilot and crew he took off in a RAF Sea King helicopter. The thermal camera was fitted underneath the helicopter but controlled from the inside. Matt used the camera by remote control. By the end of the day Matt was pretty happy using the kit, and for fun we winched him out the side of the helicopter. This is what they do on a mission over water; a member of the team is lowered to rescue the person they are looking for. You can't be scared of heights and do this job!

The tricks of the trade

1. Keep the image wide to start with.

2. Look for something you can zoom in on.

3. Zoom in slowly so that you don't lose what you are focusing on.

4. Not all white things you see are people; other mammals like cows, deer and seals also show up as white blobs!

What Matt didn't realize was that he was now going to take a thermal camera to Canada. The camera was going to be used to film one of nature's most amazing spectacles: hundreds of thousands of garter snakes leaving their dens after hibernating.

MISSION IN CANADA – FIND AND FILM EMERGING GARTER SNAKES!

Boarding Pass

getting to Manitoba

WINNIPEG
NORTH AMERICA
TORONTO
LONDON
EUROPE
ASIA
AFRICA
AUSTRALASIA

Canada is massive! It is the second largest country in the world. It takes the same time to fly from England to the east coast of Canada as it does to fly across Canada itself.

WHERE WE STAYED

We stayed in some really cool hotels. One was right next to a massive frozen lake and one was a remote house, on Riding Mountain, which had a beavers' lodge in the back garden.

a beaver

A BIT ABOUT CANADA

Canada has masses of lakes and rivers which contain almost twenty per cent of the world's fresh water. In a part of Canada called Quebec, people speak French. It can get very cold and large parts of Canada are always covered in snow. It is a great place to see wildlife.

Greetings from
Canada

a black bear

Creatures that Matt saw in Canada

- Black bears – these are not all black, some are brown and some even golden!
- Canadian geese – we also get these geese in the UK.
- White buffalo – only one in every 15 million buffalo is born white!
- Moose – the world's largest deer has massive antlers and loves eating water plants.

SNAKE DENS

The Narcisse snake dens are three large sites that are well protected. In the winter over 100,000 garter snakes can be found nestling inside them. Reptiles are cold-blooded, so need to warm up before they can hunt and breed. They can do this using the sun, but the LIFE team wanted to film some really sneaky snakes.

garter snakes

Facts about garter snakes

✻ They are cold-blooded reptiles that can't generate their own heat to stay warm like we do. They need the sun or each other to stay warm. Garter snakes are the most northern snakes in the Americas – they live where it gets seriously cold!

✻ Garter snakes huddle together underground to hibernate. It's snowy outside so they don't waste energy looking for food.

✻ When the spring comes and it gets warmer, the snakes start to leave the den.

✻ The first snakes to emerge are all males. They want to get warm before the females emerge. Snakes that are cold can't move very fast, they need energy to move quickly!

✻ Leaving the nest can be dangerous, birds are on the look-out.

✻ The only way to see what is going on is by using a thermal imaging camera.

garter snakes

nest

In these numbers, it's a good thing they are not venomous!

FILMING THE SNAKES

Matt helped top wildlife cameraman Gavin Thurston and the LIFE crew film garter snakes with the thermal camera. By using the thermal camera, Matt was able to see what was going on in the snakes' world – he could see which were hottest and how they managed to steal heat from each other by forming massive snake balls. The snakes slithering all over each other made a weird noise like leaves rustling.

best mates!

SNAKE SURPRISE!

Matt travelled to some snake dens in a top-secret LIFE location. It was really hot there so the snakes were moving more quickly and thousands more had come out of their dens – there were tens of thousands slithering over the ground and over our feet – some snakes got confused and tried to cosy up with the camera tripods!

MISSION: COMPLETED!

GOBIES

MISSION:
Gobies

AGENT:
Jacob

ALIAS:
Jake

BRECON BEACONS

Waterfalls in Wales are wet, very wet. And filming at the end of the winter in the damp surroundings of the Brecon Beacons National Park makes you wonder why anyone would want to work in telly. But Jacob had an important mission. He was meeting up with wildlife cameraman Gavin Thurston, who was testing out a piece of equipment that would be able to carry a camera back and forth over fast flowing torrents. It provides really smooth shots over water without the camera operator having to get wet. At least, that's the plan.

Jacob was keen to help out with this test run but he was going to get a soaking on this mission in more ways than one! →

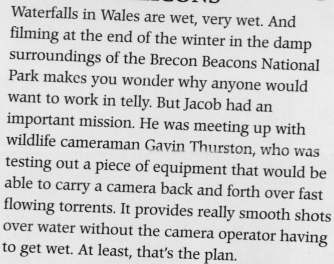

CABLE DOLLY

The idea is that the cable stretches tight like a washing line over the water and you need to find a place where you can hitch either end onto trees. The trees have to be very strong to take the tension and they need to be high enough so that the cable doesn't sag and get the camera wet.

positioning the cable

MISSION: IN UK – FIND OUT HOW TO SEND A CAMERA UP A WATERFALL

PRACTICE RUN

The LIFE team attached a lightweight camera to the cable and the dolly. The best part was using the radio controls to operate it from a distance – a bit like driving a remote control car. Luckily the expensive camera didn't fall into the water and after a few wobbles they managed to get a smooth run.

Once Jacob had mastered all of the equipment, he was told he would be taking the cable dolly to the LIFE crew who were filming at a secret location in Hawaii.

One variety of the goby has hidden talents – it can climb up waterfalls!

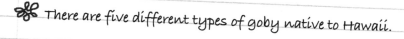

Hawaiian Goby – The Facts

❀ There are five different types of goby native to Hawaii.

❀ They range from olive to brown in colour.

❀ Adult gobies are only about five or eight centimetres long.

❀ These little fish eat small algae and other tiny animals living in the water.

❀ Gobies have special adaptations which mean they can climb up vertical waterfalls.

❀ O'opu 'alamo'o is a rare species of goby that can climb the highest waterfalls. The name means 'lizard-like' as this fish looks a bit reptilian.

❀ One goby can lay around 12,000 eggs at a time in Hawaii's great waterfalls.

❀ Their eggs get washed down the falls and out into the sea, hatching just two or three days later.

❀ Gobies are freshwater fish but they start their life in the ocean.

❀ As baby fish they have a strong instinctive urge to swim against the tide which takes them inland up rivers.

❀ They are preyed on by large numbers of bigger fish that live in the sea and in the rivers.

❀ Some Hawaiian gobies are seen as symbols of good luck.

MISSION: IN HAWAII – DELIVER THE CABLE TO THE LIFE TEAM AND FIND OUT HOW TO FILM AN AMAZING WATERFALL CLIMBING FISH

Hawaii

Boarding Pass

LONDON

NORTH AMERICA

BIG ISLAND

EUROPE

ASIA

AFRICA

no telly ... boring!

GETTING THERE

Big Island is the biggest of all the islands that make up the US state of Hawaii. From London it's a whopping 7,200 air miles and that's about 17 hours on a plane seat. Jacob's TV didn't work, so he was a bit bored.

palm trees and ocean

WHERE WE STAYED

We finally got to Big Island and based ourselves in a town called Hilo. The hotel was good and so was the food – if you liked SPAM burgers! We settled into laid-back Hawaiian life, palm trees and the ocean, although there wasn't that much time to relax as there was lots of filming to do!

A BIT ABOUT HAWAII

Hawaii is one of the most remote places on earth and well known for its big surf and hula dancing. The islands of Hawaii are the result of huge amounts of lava being spewed out of the ocean floor. Each island is made up of volcanoes. Creating this chain of peaks kicked off about five million years ago, but when Jacob arrived on Big Island things hadn't exactly settled down!

A BIT ABOUT BIG ISLAND

Big Island looks like paradise, but beneath the earth's surface there are plenty of rumbles and grumbles. Parts of the island are subjected to volcanic lava flows and toxic fumes. One day you can be baking in the sun, the next choking on fumes with dusty ash falling from the sky. Why? Well, its main volcano is Kilauea, millions of years in the making. This massive mountain is the world's most active volcano and known for its spectacular flows of molten lava.

On some parts of the island the old lava has settled and hardened, creating a very barren landscape so it's a bit like being on the moon.

SEA LIFE

If Jacob was going to experience life in this marine world, then he would have to venture underwater himself. One way to explore Hawaii's amazing sea life is to snorkel. At night it was even more exciting to snorkel as manta rays glided like spaceships through the water. If you were a goby, then these creatures would seem like giants. And there are plenty of sharks cruising around Hawaii's coastline too. Thankfully, on this underwater adventure Jacob didn't have the pleasure of bumping into one.

turtle

manta ray

VOLCANOES

When the earth's tectonic plates started shuffling about around five and a half million years ago, they hit a hotspot that produced enough lava out of the ocean floor to build the chain of islands that make up Hawaii. Today Big Island sits on that hotspot, so each day there is some volcanic activity on Mount Kilauea. Every day tiny earthquakes are recorded, and occasionally a large one even rocks the island.

VOG!

Volcanic smog is called vog. It's a mixture of sulphuric gases and other toxic fumes that roll around in a fog. It stings your eyes and can give you severe breathing problems.

HAWAII – AN UNPREDICTABLE PLACE TO FILM

When you think of Hawaii, I guess the first things that spring to mind are the funky shirts and stretches of beach with crashing surf. Those things exist but there was another side to the place . . .

can we go now?!

MOODY VOLCANO

Mount Kilauea, which is one of Hawaii's active volcanoes, suddenly became very active when we got there. The plan was to explore and film around this volcano, but as we headed up the hillside we were engulfed in thick grey, smoky fog. As we got nearer to the top of the volcano, we realised that we were right in the centre of vog! Further up, the gates to the National Park were closed. It would be days until they would be open again, putting Jacob and the crew's schedule into a right muddle.

RAIN, RAIN, RAIN . . .

In Hawaii it's not just a moody volcano that you have to contend with. Like any luscious green place, the islands attract a lot of rain. And when it rains it pours! While the rains continued to fall, filming was delayed further, putting even more pressure on Jacob and the LIFE team.

CLIMBING WATERFALLS

Eventually the rain stopped and Jacob could focus on the gobies and their incredible journey. In order to find out just how extreme their migration is, we sent him off to climb a waterfall. Fish carry out this watery expedition for survival. Because of the possibility of flash flooding, every moment on the waterfall was a nervous one. The team constantly had their eye on the water levels. Anyone washed down the face of the waterfall in a flash flood was likely to be killed.

waterfall

the LIFE Team

LIFE TEAM AND THE CABLE DOLLY

The LIFE team were in Hawaii to put together a film sequence telling the story of the gobies' mammoth journey. They wanted to show the amazing climb up the waterfalls and get shots from the gobies' point of view. This is where the team needed the cable dolly. Jacob had travelled halfway around the world with this piece of specialist equipment and now he was ready to deliver it to the team. The LIFE team were up the mountain where the waterfall was at its strongest. It was a relief to reach the top and make the drop with the film crew. They would now be able to start the delicate process of filming this fabulous fish.

MISSION: COMPLETED!

BUILDING A REEF

TESTING THE EQUIPMENT

James met up with Mike Pitts and David Jones in a swimming pool just outside Bath. His mission was to help the LIFE team test some underwater camera gear before it was used for filming. If there were any leaks or damage to the equipment, it meant they could fix it in the UK rather than have to get someone to fly out and fix it wherever they were using it in the world.

TOP SECRET

MISSION: Building a reef
AGENT: James
ALIAS: James

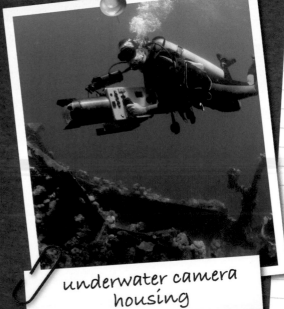

underwater camera housing

Underwater Cameras

❧ Normal cameras are put into watertight cases.

❧ These cases are called 'housings'.

❧ These housings have a rubber seal so that water doesn't get in.

❧ Each different shaped camera has its own specific housing.

❧ When you are in the water with them, it is tricky to get to the buttons.

MISSION: IN UK — TEST SOME UNDERWATER CAMERA EQUIPMENT

Great Barrier Reef

Reefs

❀ Reefs are living things, primarily made of coral.

❀ Coral is not a plant or a rock, but an animal!

❀ The largest reef in the world is the Great Barrier Reef in Australia.

❀ Reefs are home to loads of animals. They are as bursting with life as the biggest rainforests.

coral reef formation

TEST TRIAL

Luckily, the camera didn't leak! And while the LIFE team continued to test the rest of the kit, David and Mike were setting up a surprise for James. They had written James' mission on an underwater board in the deep end of the pool. James was going to accompany this kit to its next destination. The Bahamas!

The LIFE team wanted to film the birth of a new reef, and they had planned a very special way of doing this.

Caribbean reef shark

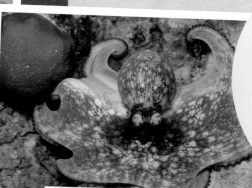

Caribbean reef octopus

MISSION: IN BAHAMAS – HELP FILM THE FORMING OF A NEW REEF

Boarding Pass

NORTH AMERICA

LONDON

ASIA

EUROPE

BAHAMAS

AFRICA

SOUTH AMERICA

AUSTRALASIA

ABOUT THE BAHAMAS

The Bahamas are a group of tropical islands in the Caribbean, only a few kilometres off the coast of America. These islands are famous for all their wonderful reefs and diving. Loads of James Bond scenes have been filmed in the Bahamas.

These islands have no fresh water so, every day a huge tanker sails in from America full of water.

Paradise Island, Bahamas

THE PLAN

The plan was simple. The LIFE team led by producer Neil Lucas were going to sink a boat – on purpose! Sunken wrecks are exactly what the small microscopic creatures that float in the sea are looking for. Once they find one they quickly colonize it. Finding space in an established coral reef is impossible. So a sunken boat is quickly covered in new life, and over the next three years the LIFE team wanted to film the wreck at different stages to show how a reef forms.

ready to sink!

...not yet!

THE PROBLEM

A change in government meant that the papers the LIFE team had were useless. They had to reapply and that would take a while. James and the Inside LIFE team left the island before seeing the boat sink. Mission failed!

THE SOLUTION

Later that year, James heard that the LIFE team had managed to sink the boat and it was now sitting on the bottom of the ocean in the Bahamas. He wanted to see it – but first he'd need to learn how to dive. He contacted David Jones, a diving instructor, and paid him a visit.

SCUBA diving is when you use special air in tanks to breathe underwater.

SCUBA actually stands for **Self Contained Underwater Breathing Apparatus.**

MISSION: IN BAHAMAS – HELP FILM
THE FORMING OF A NEW REEF

ALMOST A YEAR LATER

James returned to the Bahamas with the LIFE team. The LIFE team needed to film the wreck to see how the reef had been developing. James was going to go underwater to see it for the first time.

PRACTICE DIVES

But before he could he had to do some practice dives.

After a few trial runs James proved that he could dive. He finally got the go-ahead to take the plunge and explore the LIFE team's wreck.

scuba diver

SUCCESS!

While he was down in the wreck, the LIFE team managed to film all sorts of new animals living and growing there. It was a real success! And an example of the lengths the BBC go to, to capture these amazing images.

In ten years' time the wreck will still be there with coral and anemones, sea slugs and fish making it a home.

The LIFE team hope that the reef will become full of new life like: Caribbean reef sharks, tiger groupers, Nassau groupers, corals, anemones, hydroids, banded coral shrimps, arrow crabs, Caribbean reef octopuses, surgeon fish, moray eels . . .

convict surgeon fish

moray eel

arrow crab

banded coral shrimp

tiger grouper

corals

Nassau grouper

reef shark

reef octopus

giant anemone

MISSION: COMPLETED!

GOODBYE FROM

INSIDE LIFE

Inside LIFE is the first of its kind, a children's show that is involved with a huge wildlife series for BBC One. When we first broached the idea with CBBC, everyone instantly wondered why we hadn't done this before. Sometimes the most obvious ideas are the best.

As we grew up, the natural world was a magical world, full of surprise and intrigue, murder and mystery, new things and shocking things, and as we get older, this world becomes even more magical, even more shocking and even more surprising every single day.

Don't believe us? Well, how about this . . .

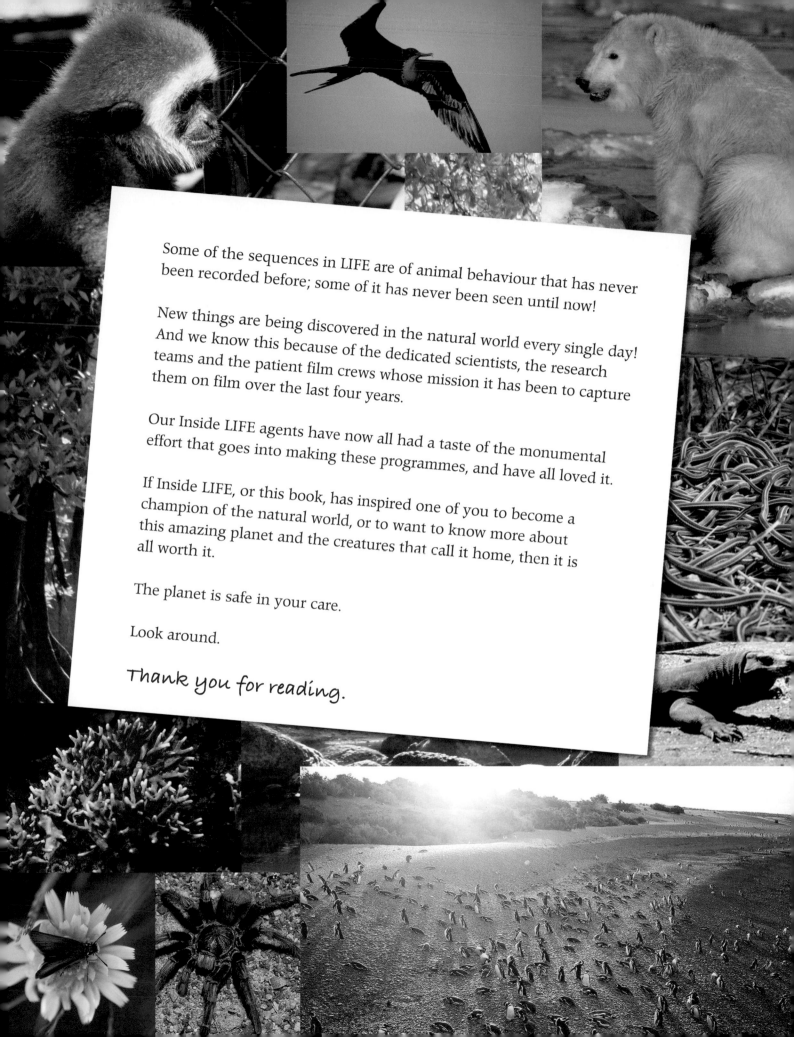

Some of the sequences in LIFE are of animal behaviour that has never been recorded before; some of it has never been seen until now!

New things are being discovered in the natural world every single day! And we know this because of the dedicated scientists, the research teams and the patient film crews whose mission it has been to capture them on film over the last four years.

Our Inside LIFE agents have now all had a taste of the monumental effort that goes into making these programmes, and have all loved it.

If Inside LIFE, or this book, has inspired one of you to become a champion of the natural world, or to want to know more about this amazing planet and the creatures that call it home, then it is all worth it.

The planet is safe in your care.

Look around.

Thank you for reading.

GOODBYE FROM

JAMES jumped into a pool in Bath and climbed out of the ocean in the Bahamas after having fun with speed boats, sharks and submarines!

SCARLET was lucky enough to see one of the Eight Wonders of the World, the Taj Mahal. She also got to see a wild tiger!

BILLY not only got to witness lemurs behaving badly, but he also got to hang out with them!

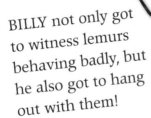

GREGORY landed safe and sound. His verdict: helicopters are great! Much better than boats!

LOUISE survived sub-zero temperatures and an encounter with the world's largest carnivore.

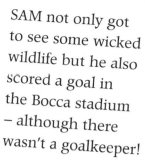

SAM not only got to see some wicked wildlife but he also scored a goal in the Bocca stadium – although there wasn't a goalkeeper!

IZZY had her birthday floating on the sea next to an island full of dragons!

BRYONY scaled the treetops with a troop of gibbons, and came down completely unscathed.

JACOB got rained on in Hawaii – he also luckily just missed an erupting volcano.

MATT found himself in the middle of nowhere, surrounded by hundreds of thousands of snakes, and he loved it!

INDEX

PICTURE CREDITS

Front cover images:
Doug Hope
Chris Howard
Tom Jarvis
Mandi Stark
Emily Winks

Back cover images:
Tom Clarke
Doug Hope
Chris Howard
Tom Jarvis
Graham Macfarlane
Kate Markham
Michael Pitts
Lisanne O'Keefe
Mandi Stark
Jerry Short
Emily Winks
Andrew Yarme

Inside images:
John Aitchison – 63br, 67r

Simon Blakeney – 22l

Tom Clarke – 18r, 20bl, 21tl, 21tr, 21br, 22l, 22r, 23tr, 23b, 25b, 56bl

Simon Cole – 2tr, 16bl, 20t, 25tr, 74r, 76r, 78bl, 79br, 89bl, 94tr

Doug Hope – 2l, 2bl, 10tr, 11br, 12, 12bl, 15tl, 17bl, 17br, 19l, 20tr, 20r, 21r, 24bl, 25ml, 26tl, 27tl, 27b, 28b, 29bl, 29br, 30t, 30l, 30b, 31t, 31r, 31b, 32t, 34b, 35t, 35t, 35t, 35t, 35t, 35b, 37, 46br, 47tl, 48tr, 48l, 48r, 86tr, 87br, 89tl, 94l, 94bl

Chris Howard – 2tr, 2r, 11tl, 11m, 12, 15r, 17r, 17r, 20tl, 20br, 21bl, 24br, 50tl, 51tl, 53, 53br, 54t, 54br, 55tr, 55l, 55bl, 87tl, 87m, 89, 94tr, 94r

Tom Jarvis – 2r, 2br, 7, 11tr, 13br, 14br, 16tl, 16tl, 19tr, 25tl, 38tl, 38r, 39tl, 40r, 40br, 41tr, 41tr, 41tr, 41tr, 42tr, 42l, 42bl, 43t, 43r, 87tr, 88br, 93, 94br, 94br

Miranda Lippiatt – 2b, 14, 17bl, 25r, 84tr, 88, 94b

Stephen Lyle – 56b, 57tr, 94t

Graham Macfarlane – 3r, 13tl, 14tl, 16tr, 21l, 21b, 24l, 44tl, 45tr, 47l, 49tl, 49b, 89tr, 95r

Kate Markham – 2r, 10ml, 10m, 12bm, 15bl, 16bl, 20tlm, 74tl, 74br, 75bl, 76bl, 77tr, 77, 79tr, 86lm, 86m, 94r

Sean Miller – 10bl, 86bl

Lisanne O'Keefe – 3b, 13bl, 14tr, 17, 62tl, 62r, 65br, 88tr, 95b

Michael Pitts – 23r, 80bl

Mark Roberts – 20ml, 50r, 52r, 53b, 53t

Adam Scott – 22tr, 22b, 23tl, 48bl, 54b, 55br

Jerry Short – 2t, 10t, 12br, 14bl, 16b, 19br, 24tl, 24tr, 56tl, 56br, 57, 57br, 58bl, 59l, 59br, 60l, 64l, 64r, 86t, 88bl

Mandi Stark – 3l, 3, 11mr, 13b, 15br, 16, 16, 25bl, 60tl, 69tr, 71br, 72tr, 72br, 73, 73br, 87rm, 89br, 95l, 95

Emily Winks – 3bl, 8bl, 10l, 20, 20m, 25l, 25bl, 65l, 66b, 66t, 67t, 67br, 86l, 95bl

Andrew Yarme – 3tl, 13tr, 14tr, 16l, 80tr, 83tr, 83r, 88tl, 95tl